Ouija Board 101: A Short Guide On Safely Using Your Board

By Nicholas Hawthorn

CW00952473

Disclaimer

Introduction

In this short but precise book you will find the most frequently asked questions on Ouija Boards answered. You'll discover the basics on how to safely and properly use your board for maximum effectiveness. This book isn't for the advanced or experienced Ouija Board enthusiast, but rather for someone who is using it for the first time and needs a quick guide to getting started.

The book covers the popular questions someone may ask about using a Ouija Board.

"A friend comes over with a Ouija board.
It spells out: Bourbon. Where's the band?

Just because you're dead doesn't mean you can't have fun."

— *Kelli Russell Agodon, Hourglass Museum*

Chapter 1: The History of The Ouija Board

The Ouija Board or also know as a spirit/talking board is typically a wooden board. This wooden board generally has the alphabet from A-Z and numbers with 1-9, It will also have **YES** or **No** in the top corners and a **Goodbye** at the bottom.

With the board there will be a wooden Planchette piece that's shaped like a heart. This is the piece that will be used by any participants. These planchettes are normally plain but you can also get some custom designed with cool designs.

Changchun Temple Master and disciples painting. Photo by Vmenkov.

The first documented uses of the Ouija or Automatic Writing were in China, around 1100 AD. This information is highlighted in the Song Dynasty's historical documents. They referred to it as *Fuji (扶乩)*. *Or in English, planchette writing.*

Back then it was a possible means of contacting the dead or the other side. Under rituals and supervision it became a central practice of the Quanzhen School until it was later forbidden by the Qing Dynasty.

Fast forward a few centuries to 1886, the art of Spiritualism or the belief that we could talk to the dead became very popular and fast growing.

Over the next couple of years talking boards were created to fill the need that people wanted. Then came along a particular businessman called Elijah Bond, Elijah Bond had the idea to patent a board with a planchette that had the alphabet and some numbers printed on it. On February 10th 1891 the patent protection was approved and the particular patent they received was U.S. Patent 446,054.

In 1901 an employee of Elijah's, named William Fuld took over the production of talking boards and started his own version called "Ouija". A man by the name of Charles Kennard who was the founder of Kennard Novelty (the company who manufactured the boards) claimed he was told the name "Ouija" from using a board and that it was an Egyptian word meaning "good luck".

This name came from the French and German word "yes" put together.

French - *Oui*

-Ouija

German - *Ja*

Media & Notables

Even though originally it was only meant to be a parlour game or fun toy for people to use, stories started to emerge of peculiar things happening such as paranormal activity.

Various notable people have used the board such as Dick Brooks of the Houdini Museum in Pennsylvania. He used the Board as part of a paranormal seance presentation.

- In 1893 G. K. Chesterton used the Ouija Board when he had depression and skepticism and eventually grew fascinated with the occult.

- Vincent Damon Furnier the vocalist of band Alice Cooper which later he adopted the name when he went solo. He got the name from a session with the Ouija Board.

- The poet James Merrill also used the board for years and he even wanted the spirits to enter his body. Before he unfortunately passed away, he urged people to not use Ouija Boards!

- In London of 1994 a convicted murder named Stephen

Young was allowed a retrial after four of the jurors held a séance and had apparently contacted the murdered man. This spirit went on to say that young was the murderer and eventually young was convicted a second time and was jailed for life. Read the Ouija Case here.

Photo Taken by Jorge Figueroa

Over the years many things have been produced on the topic of the Ouija Board, films such as *Ouija, A Haunted House* and *A Haunting - Black Magic*.

Many books and also things such as phone covers and mouse mats have been produced to sell to believers and fans of this spooky board.

Chapter 2: Getting Started With A Ouija Board.

When we deal with the Ouija Board there is *3 main rules* you always need to abide by and always DO. IF you follow these rules you will increase the chances of safe communication.

1. **ALWAYS say GOODBYE at the end of a session.** - If you don't do this then Spirits and Demons will refuse to leave and will stay there even after you've closed the board. Obviously not all spirits are

the same but if you do get a malevolent one that refuses to go. You will have to make them leave by forcibly moving the planchette to GOODBYE. It's a bit like leading a stubborn child away from a store with some sweets.

2. **Be SERIOUS** - When you are having a session with the Ouija Board always take it seriously. Even though I explained in the beginning Chapter that the Ouija Board was a Parlour game, It should never be taken as a game! Don't mess around and make sure you are prepared for any negative energy to come your way.

3. **Never use in your own home** - If at all possible try not to have a Ouija Board session in your home! If something goes wrong any spirits can linger and cause havoc in your daily lives and mess with your family. You want you home to be a sanctum and a place of rest.

Ok now we have those 3 main rules out-of-the-way I will tell you how to conduct a session with the Ouija Board.

Ouija Board Instructions & Dangers

If you want to do this properly then make sure you follow my instructions properly.

Roles

Typically a session involves 3-5 people. So once you have gathered preferably 5 people, you'll need to assign roles. There will be a Leader, Document Keeper and 3 Participants (or energizers).

Leader - The Leader will be the one to take control and have one finger on the planchette. He/She will ask the questions and be the one talking and dictating the pace.

Document Keeper - The Document Keeper will be sitting back and watching the session unfold. He/She will be taking notes and writing down what the board spells out.

3 Participants - The 3 participants will be the ones who will channeling their energy and focusing on the board. They each will have a finger on the planchette and will be focusing on the task at hand.

Before you start off communicating with the Ouija Board, everyone has to know their roles. Make sure everyone is focused and calm. You are all working as a team and If just one person isn't focused or calm, then you'll have less success with communication and things will go slower, or not at all.

Starting The Communication

Normally the best time to have Ouija Session is after 10:00pm, as this is when the spirits are more active.

When starting off make sure you are in a quiet area and are comfortable, this will allow for concentration and focus. Place the board either on a flat and steady table or your knees(depending how many of you there are). Make sure your arms aren't at an awkward angle and you can reach the planchette freely.

All participants need to gently put their finger on the planchette or glass (document keeper doesn't have to) and clear their mind of negative thoughts. Then all the participants need to channel their focus and energy towards the planchette. If done right, the planchette should start to move either slow, fast or dart across the board every now and again.

If everyone is focusing, calm and comfortable and the planchette still isn't moving, It could be asleep so gently move it in circles (manually move it yourself). Then try luring a spirit in by saying sentences like "Spirit, this is a safe place" or "Is there a spirit with a message for someone at this table?" The aim is to try to get the spirit to talk to you.

Remember that the aim is to get the planchette to move on its own free will and not move it yourself.

If these sentences don't work then try switching roles as Leader. Once the planchette starts to move on its own, we can start with the communication.

Great Questions to Ask

Once you have established communication on the Ouija Board you can start asking some basic questions such as:

- The spirit's name

- The spirits Age when he/she died

- The spirits date of Death

- The spirits Gender

Once these are answered you can move on to more of the in-depth questions like:

- How they died

- Do they have a message for anyone in the group

- Is there anything they want from a living person

Remember you can ask them anything, It's like talking to a person but they are kind of dead. When communicating just be sincere and polite.

Closing The Board

Once you are finished you are going to need to close the board. Remember back to our 3 rules at the beginning? When you are finishing up remember to always say goodbye to the spirit and wish them peace and the spirit should then guide the planchette to the Goodbye on the board.

As explained earlier on. If you don't do this you'll leave the door for any old spirit to walk through. Whether it be negative or good.

When To & How To Close The Board

Sometimes you may need to close the board early and say goodbye. If the following happens try to end the session with good-bye as soon as possible.

- The room becomes dark, heavy and filled with negative energy.

- The spirit starts swearing or becoming agitated

- Things start to become erratic in the room

Sometimes the spirit will refuse to say goodbye so in a sterner tone of voice you say "I'm saying GOODBYE and I wish for you to do the same please!" If they still don't move it to goodbye then calmly force the planchette to the goodbye.

In a sterner voice then say "GOODBYE and LEAVE" out loud. Remove the planchette from the board and slam it down (not too hard)to break connection. Whilst remaining calm quickly get out of the room.

At the end of the day a Ouija Board even though designed as a game, is far from one. This can be quite taxing on yourselves and the spirits so make sure you try to limit any use to below an hour and a half.

Also the more you use a Ouija Board/Talking Board the more success you will have in the future.

Chapter 3: The Top 5 Tips When Using A Ouija Board

In this chapter you will be provided with my top 5 tips you can apply when using a *Ouija Board*. These tips will help to make your Ouija Board session, safer and more of a pleasant experience.

1. Respect The Board

Even though the board was originally meant as a game, it is far from one. When you are participating in a session, try not to mess around. Or disrespect the spirits, people in the room or the board. This can lead to negative spirits entering the room or **no** spirits showing up at all!

Obviously you can have fun and laugh every now and again because laughing can sometimes bring spirits in. But try to strike a happy medium when it comes to the atmosphere and focus.

If you respect the board and sessions you'll more of a chance of communication and more of the chance you'll encounter positive spirits.

2. Never Play Alone

Unless you are a master of your energy and have the brain to handle spirits, most of the time It's *unwise* to play alone. When you play alone It's very hard for you to contact spirits, this is why It's good practice to do it with at-least 2-5 people. Even If it's just two people, one can ask questions and the other can solely focus their energy on the planchette and board.

By the off-chance you do encounter communication, It will be hard for you to control anything if something does happen on your own. If you are with a few other people, bad spirits are less likely to cross-over.

3. Have Patience

Sometimes when you are playing the Ouija board It can become frustrating when the board does nothing. Or when the spirits are messing around with you.

This is when you are going to need patience.

If you can't establish contact that session, say goodbye and come back to it another day. With patience and practice you will start seeing results. In no time you'll be having fun and contacting the other side!

4. Be Polite

As well as in the daily life of an alive human being, everyone likes to be spoken to politely and with respect, no? Well I know that I *do*! So the same will apply to people who aren't with us anymore.

When you are asking questions, try to ask them politely and say things like

"thanks for answering our questions".
Another example is "we are saying
goodbye now, we wish you peace and
thank you".

Being polite will please the spirits and
have a higher chance of not making
them angry.

5. Know When To End

Last but not least is my final tip, Number
5. This is perhaps one of the most
important ones...you have to know when
to end a session.

Even though you don't want to contact
anything evil. There is a likely chance
you will. So when you do encounter
something evil you need to know when
to end the session.

If the following things happen make sure you push the planchette to Goodbye and say Goodbye. Then promptly remove the planchette and slam it down off the board (not too hard though). Flip the board over, turn on any lights and leave the room!

- The spirit starts to spell out an evil word like, **'HELL'**, **'DEMON', 'DEATH', 'SATAN', 'TRICKSTER', 'LUCIFER'**, etc. If this happens stop it from spelling out the word mid way.

- The spirit starts doing figure of eights.

- The spirit starts to go to each four corners of the board. If this happens there's a chance the spirit will escape the board.

- The spirit starts to go through the numbers and alphabet like 1, 2, 3, 4, or a, b, c, d as with the four corners, if the spirit is allowed to go from start to finish the spirit can escape.

- Any spirit starts swearing or becoming hostile.

If any of the above things happen just do as I explained and you'll be **OK**.

Chapter 4: Ouija Board Sessions On Halloween

Normally using your Ouija Board at the best of time is *risky* business. The only other day where using it could be more risky is on Halloween.

What Is Halloween?

Halloween or Hallows-Evening is a Holiday which comes around each year on the 31st of October.

This day, starts the 3 day-observance of Allhallowtide. In this time we celebrate the dead including, Saints, Martyrs and the believers. A lot of people believe that Halloween actually comes from the Celtic Festival of Samhain. When people would light bonfires, wear masks and ward off ghosts and evil spirits.

Why Should You Be Careful On Halloween With Your Ouija Board?

If you haven't guessed already Halloween is the eve of celebrating the days of the dead, so around this time ghosts, evil spirits and demons are more active.

If you don't know what you are doing this can lead to some unwanted visitors in your home! Or worse in your friends or family! As well as you increasing the likelihood of you contacting spirits there

is an increased chance of around 50%
you can become possessed.

*Fun Fact: On Halloween the amount
of ghost activity increases by 30%*

Tips & Precautions

Now you have a few facts and numbers,
It's time i showed you some ways to
either fend off evil spirits or make your
Ouija Board Session more exciting!

1. If you are going out, cut up 9
   round pieces of orange peel
   from one orange. You can
   carry these around with you in
   your pocket. In the east 9 is
   considered a lucky number
   and the strong scent of
   orange will keep you alert. As

well as bright orange being a colour of protection.

2. Carve out some Jack O-Lanterns. Carve out some pumpkins and put a candle inside. These will ward of some evil spirits from your home. Try and put them on your doorsteps or near your doors.

3. Light a bonfire. Lighting a bonfire will keep a bright light and ward off any evil spirits or ghosts.

4. Dress Up. By dressing up you are disguising yourself and in turn misleading any ghost or spirits.

5. Hang little bells tied to your door knobs with a ribbon. This will alert you to any unwanted spirits that pass through.

6. If you go ghost hunting, don't go alone and **always** take a phone with you.

7. This is pretty much all the time but applies for Halloween too. Don't threaten or abuse ghosts or spirits. This can lead to some bad consequences!

8. Eat plenty of food including vegetables and fruits. Drink apple cider and plenty of wine and have fun.

As long as you follow Chapter 2 & Chapter 3, you'll be fine, just be that little more vigilant and ask simple and safe questions.

Chapter 5: Ouija Board Sessions On Diwali

Diwali "The festival of lights" is an ancient Hindu festival. It is celebrated in autumn (northern hemisphere) or in spring (southern hemisphere) and Diwali is one of the most biggest and brightest of festivals in India.

The actual festival signifies and celebrates the victory over evil, typically the rituals and preparations last over a 5 day period. The main event or festival night though, occurs on darkest new

moon night of the Hindu Lunisolar
month Kartika.

In the Gregorian calendar, Diwali falls
between mid-October and mid-
November.

Before Diwali night, Hindus tend to
clean, renovate and decorate their
homes and offices. Then on the night of
Diwali, people will dress up in their best
clothes and light up *diyas* (lamps and
candles) inside and outside of their
homes.

They participate in family *puja* (prayers),
typically to the goddess of wealth and
prosperity - Lakshmi. After Puja,
fireworks are set off then a family feast
occurs, normally including *mithai*

(sweets), after the feast gifts are exchanged a little bit like Christmas.

The Story Of Diwali

Once upon a time there was a great warrior, Prince Rama, who had a beautiful wife named Sita.

There was also a terrible demon king, Ravana. He had twenty arms and ten heads, and was feared throughout the land. He wanted to make Sita his wife, and one day he kidnapped her and took her away in his chariot. Clever Sita left a trail of her jewellery for Rama to follow.

Rama followed the trail of glittering jewellery until he met the monkey king, Hanuman, who became his friend and agreed to help find Sita. Messages were sent to all the monkeys in the world, and through them to all the bears, who set out to find Sita.

After a very long search, Hanuman found Sita imprisoned on an island. Rama's army of monkeys and bears couldn't reach the island, so they began to build a bridge. Soon all the animals of the world, large and small, came to help. When the bridge was built, they rushed across it and fought a mighty battle.

When Rama killed the evil Ravana with a magic arrow, the whole world rejoiced. Rama and Sita began their long journey back to their land, and everybody lit oil lamps to guide them on their way and welcome them back.

Ever since, people light lamps at Diwali to remember that light triumphs over dark and good triumphs over evil.

Are There Any Major Risks Using Your Ouija Board On Diwali?

So the question is, are there any risks when using your Ouija board on Diwali?

Short answer is No.

Unlike Halloween, there is so much positive energy floating around on Diwali it will be really hard to contact any evil spirits. Do expect to contact various friendly spirits though. Due to the increased energy the festival produces, you'll more than likely will contact someone.

Chapter 6: Ouija Board Sessions On Friday The 13th

In western superstition Friday 13th is considered an *unlucky* day. It occurs when the 13th day of a month falls on a Friday in the Gregorian calendar. It is also known as Black Friday.

The fear of the number 13 has an actual name called, triskaidekaphobia!

The superstition may have of arose from the middle ages. Originating from the story of Jesus Christ's last supper and crucifixion. In which there were 13 individuals present in the Upper Room on the 13th of Nisan Maundy Thursday, the night before his death on Good Friday.

Also an early documented reference in English occurs in Henry Sutherland Edwards' 1869 biography of Gioachino Rossini, who died on Friday 13th.

He [Rossini] was surrounded to the last by admiring friends; and if it be true that, like so many Italians, he regarded Fridays as an unlucky day and thirteen as an unlucky number, it is remarkable that on Friday 13th of November he passed away.

Now it's the modern age, many films and fiction novels have been built upon the superstition that arises from this day. Including the famous films of Jason Vorhees preying on helpless campers.

Using Your Ouija Board On Friday 13th

Now down to our normal discussion in regards to using your Ouija Board! When It comes to Friday the 13th, If you believe in the Ouija Board you may also believe in Friday 13th.

Even though Friday 13th is a really unlucky day, you shouldn't need to worry about using your Ouija board. But depending on the circumstances, you may be so unlucky that you don't actually contact anyone via the Ouija Board.

So It's totally down to your own preferences whether you attempt to waste your energy on Friday 13th or not.

Just remember though that approaching the board with negative or fearful emotions can do more harm than good, and it **can** attract the same sort of emotions from the things you contact!

If today makes you too fearful and/or harbour too many emotions for you, then don't do it. Leave it and approach the board with a clear head at a later date.

If you do plan to have a session today though, just make sure you go into the session with a fearless and loving mindset. Don't go into the session with the opposite or it could mess up the session or your own mental stability.

Chapter 7: 666 & Your Ouija Board

When you hear the number 666 you automatically think of the devil, evil and the end of times, but through research and already attained knowledge. There are actually a few beliefs behind 666.

It's quite interesting actually how a whole planet fear a number like this? When In reality all it is, is a 3 digit number in which all the numbers are the same.

So In this post I'm going to go through the origin of 666, the different beliefs around the world and what to do if it spells out on the Ouija Board You're using!

666 Origins

Christianity

Let's start at the beginning and how as a human race we have come around to fear this number.

666 originally arose from a verse in the Book Of Revelation, of the New Testament and is the number of the beast. The number of the beast is mentioned in Chapter **13:18** once. This verse reads the following:

Here is wisdom. Let him that hath understanding count the number of the beast: for it is the number of a man; and his number is Six hundred threescore and six.

In Greek Manuscripts, the book of Revelation is titled the Apocalypse of John. In these, the number is rendered in Greek numerical form as χξ□. Or sometimes as ἑξακόσιοι ἑξήκοντα ἕξ,

hexakósioi hexēkonta héx "six hundred and sixty six".

This beast that is referenced as having seven heads, ten horns and which comes out of the sea.

In Chapter **13:1**, the verse reads:

The dragon stood on the shore of the sea. And I saw a beast coming out of the sea. It had ten horns and seven

*heads, with ten crowns on its horns, and
on each head a blasphemous name.*

Then In Chapter **20:2** It reads:

*He seized the dragon, that ancient
serpent, who is the devil, or Satan, and
bound him for a thousand years.*

So as you can see by the scriptures
Christians believed that the beast was a
manifestation of the Devil or Satan.

Other Christian Interpretations

In other Christian interpretations, 666
(The Beast) can also be the viewed as a
sign of the antiChrist. In short an
antiChrist is anyone who denies that
Jesus Christ is God. It is mentioned a

few times in the Bible. Such as the following in **2 John 1:7**:

I say this because many deceivers, who do not acknowledge Jesus Christ as coming in the flesh, have gone out into the world. Any such person is the deceiver and the antichrist.

Also In the following **1 John 2:18**:

Dear children, this is the last hour; and as you have heard that the antichrist is coming, even now many antichrists have come. This is how we know it is the last hour.

Gematria

666 is gematria of the Antichrist. don't know what gematria means then <u>click here</u> to find out!

666 Origin Conclusion

So As you can see the whole origin of 666 has stemmed from Greek translations In Christianity. It symbolises the number of the beast and interpretations of it, many believe it to be the Antichrist or manifestations of Satan & the Devil.

666 The Beast - William Blake (1757-1827)

Even though there have been findings that the actual number of the Beast is 616. In 2005 fragments from papyrus 115 was revealed and it was containing the earliest known version of the Book Of Revelation and discussing the number of the beast. It gave the number as 616, but many still believe the 666 is the true number of the beast.

What To Do If Your Ouija Board Spells Out 666

So we've obtained that the number 666 is the sign of the beast and of the Antichrist. Also in some cases, Satan. If your Ouija Board spells out 666 then this means more than likely a human follower of 666 or a demon is trying to come through.

Both are associated with evil entities and are not to be messed around with. If you are dealing with a demon, then their sole purpose is to gain access to a human host and cause havoc and misery in your life.

Below is what you need to do if you do encounter this situation. All of this was mentioned in the beginning chapters, but we will go over it again here.

- Stop Playing as soon as something spells out **666**, **616**, **Devil**, **Satan**, **Antichrist**, **Death** etc.

- Force the Planchette to Goodbye and say out loud "GOODBYE Spirit! We are ending this session now! We wish you peace! GOODBYE!"

- Take the planchette off the board slam it down and turn it over.

- Turn over the Ouija Board and leave the room.

The number 666 isn't as bad as people make it out to be but it's definitely not to be trifled with when it comes to a Ouija Board! So take care when playing and always be vigilant.

Conclusion

Using a Ouija Board can be either a great experience or a terrifying one, It all depends how you approach each session. The main thing to do is make sure you stay safe and have fun. Stay safe by following the instructions provided in this guide and always take care.

I hope you have some great experiences and contact your loved ones instead of evil ones.

About The Author

Nicholas Hawthorn is a writer and author from the south of England. His love for the paranormal, horror and Gothic scene is unparalleled. There isn't much he doesn't know about things such as the Ouija Board and other spooky stuff. When he was growing up he had a fascination for ghosts and other spiritual stuff, when one day he had a strange experience.

It was a cold and rainy night, when he awoke from a deep sleep he was in. Nicholas went to the bathroom and got back into bed, on his way back though it felt like he was being watched. He closed his eyes to drift back off to sleep, upon closing them he heard a shuffling sound. He slowly opened his eyes and looked towards the end of his bed. What he saw he couldn't explain, but none-other as an outline of a man's shadow.

He quickly turned on the light and nothing was there!

To this day he still thinks it was he recently passed grandfather. Since then he spent his whole life dedicated to things of the paranormal kind. In pursuit of the age old question...are ghosts real?

If you enjoyed this book, then an honest review would be hugely appreciated, thanks.

9 781530 742431